The Glorious Ordinary

*An Invitation to Study God's Word
in Your Everyday Life*

by
Sarah E. Frazer

The Glorious Ordinary

Copyright © 2016 by Sarah E. Frazer

Learn more information at: http://www.sarahefrazer.com/

ISBN-13: 978-0692815083

Contents

Introduction

There is no thrill in walking; it is the test of all the stable qualities.[1]

– Oswald Chambers

My everyday life is pretty routine. I never jet off to exotic places or even travel downtown for a job. I spend most of my days in my home, raising my children, cleaning carpets, and walking on sticky floors. I used to rush through life, planning and doing. Even our adoption was planned. Then one day I was forced to slow down. My life came to a sudden snail's pace as my plans went out the window. I was suddenly handed a new blueprint for life.

In the civil affairs office in Zhengzhou, China, the officials handed us our daughter. After fifteen months of paper chasing and the agony of waiting, we finally had her. With four layers of clothes on, she was huge. So heavy. I tried to look into her face, but she wouldn't focus or make eye contact. I handed her to my husband, and we studied her. We smiled with relief. We had her. It was over now, right?

A horrible feeling crept into my soul while we waited to fill out more paperwork. The room with no heat felt suffocating. She would not look at us. Her body was limp, like a rag doll. She was unable to even hold the weight of her head. After she ate, she began to cry, more of a soft meow. In that moment and the days following, I realized our lives would be different. Our normal life at home would change. Forever. Her medical needs were more significant than we had anticipated.

We had anticipated her to be minor-special needs. Her only diagnosis listed was "high muscle tone." We knew something was off when she arrived to us with extremely low muscle tone. In fact, she could barely sit, crawl, or even hold her head up. She drooled constantly. While playing, she never looked at the object; she only used her peripheral vision. While we were in China, we struggled. I struggled mostly. My plan for our family was slowly coming undone.

After arriving home, I was trying to survive with four children seven and under. Our new daughter needed as much help as a newborn. I had to struggle through the pain of losing my dreams, the guilt of attachment struggles, and the crying. She would scream for hours in grief. I felt so helpless. I was supposed to be her mother, but I felt like a stranger. I felt like the babysitter, and I was drowning in grief myself. When I thought about the past, it brought guilt and shame. The future only held uncertainty. What would her quality of life be? Who would take care of her when we were gone? I hated myself for resenting the whole situation, but God used it all to slow down my frantic life. I crawled through each day because I was lost. The daily life was miserable. I wanted to be able to hope in the future, but it only scared me. I wanted relief from the pressure of caring for a special needs daughter, but I felt too tired to even know where to begin. Joy and peace were completely missing from my life.

Slowly, God promises echoed in my heart. He didn't change my circumstances; He changed my perspective. In Psalm 81, the Israelites had abandoned God. God couldn't bless them, but if they returned, God promised to provide, out of their hard situation.

"But he {GOD} would feed you {His people} with the finest of the wheat, and with honey from the rock I would satisfy you." **Psalm 81:16**

For the people of Israel, it was a time of wilderness living. A time of spiritual doubting and daily hardship. I also doubted. I wondered if I knew enough or had enough love to parent our new daughter. I doubted whether I would have enough strength for my other children. I struggled just to make it through the day. In Psalm 81:16, God looked at the rocky lives of His people, and He said, *Out of these hard places I will satisfy you with honey.* Honey is used for a sweetener and for healing. God promised them sweetness and healing, even in the midst of hard circumstances. In the middle of my day, I needed a reminder that something sweet would come from this hard season. I couldn't wait until I felt joy, love, and peace again. I didn't want to wait for life to be normal. Normal was no longer a possibility.

Maybe you are struggling with adoption. Infertility. Cancer. Chronic pain. Job loss. Grief. Loneliness. Marriage. ***Don't wait for a season of normal—look for peace today.*** It is in the ordinary we find the glory of God. He is in the small things, the daily things. He is where we are. Our lives center around the 24-hour period. He is in our hours, our minutes, and even the seconds ticking along.

I have been the waiting woman. Going through the adoption process is a desperate type of waiting. I have felt the fear of the unknown. A life in limbo is filled with ups and downs and lots of hidden anxiety. I've also lived a year of unexpected hard things. It was a year of change and struggle. Parenting a child from a hard place reveals a whole lot of your own failures and shortcomings. Their hurt reveals your own hurt. I've messed up, and the dark places of my heart have come to light. I've had to confess a lot of mistakes. God is even in the darkness.

This book is about walking one day at a time. Even though walking is so *ordinary*, don't get discouraged. I understand that the deepest part of your heart just wants this hard place to be over. I ask you to walk through whatever circumstance you are facing one day at a time with me. You aren't alone and you are made to be exceptional, right here.

It does require the supernatural grace of God to live twenty-four hours in every day as a saint – to go through drudgery as a disciple, to live an ordinary, unobserved, ignored existence as a disciple of Jesus. It is inbred of us that we have to do exceptional things for God; but we have not. We have to be exceptional in the ordinary things, to be holy in mean streets, among mean people. -

Oswald Chambers My Utmost for His Highest [2]

Living a glorious ordinary life means learning how to be exceptional for God in our ordinary days.

NOTES ABOUT THE STUDY:

The secret for learning to walk in daily communion with God will be rooted in Bible study. Each chapter will be a Bible study section. Feel free to answer the questions as you read through the passage. Most of the questions are there to help you understand what the text says. The Bible study method I have used comes in part from Jen Wilkin's book, *Women of the Word: How to Study the Bible with Both Our Hearts and Our Minds*. Some of the questions, especially the interpretation and application questions, are based on her book.

You will find five days to study God's Word. It is important you follow these basic steps when studying the Bible.

1. **Understand the Text.** Most of our study time will be focused on this step. Most of the time you will spend four days trying to understand the text *without commentaries*. Avoid looking at study notes, commentaries, or other books to help you understand the text. Feel free to read the historical context from a study Bible, but avoid their opinions on a passage. This will help you form your own opinions first.

2. **Interpret the Text.** After you have a clear understanding of the passage, you will try to figure out the purpose. Why did the author write this? I would love for you to answer this question before looking in commentaries. Then, feel free to see what other people have said.

3. **Apply the Text.** Here you will ask yourself the same application question each week. What aspect of God's character has been revealed in the text? How is this character trait illustrated? How does understanding that characteristic of God change the way I should think and act? How can I better live in the daily based on these

truths? Ultimately the Bible is about God. When we know Him better, we can learn how to live.

Take time to pray before, during, and after your time in God's Word. I've included sample prayers in the appendix for you to use.

I hope you will discover joy as you study the scripture. I hope you see His love for you in the pages of His book. Consider this your invitation to begin walking today. Not running ahead. Not sitting still. Just moving forward, one day at a time.

That God cares enough about us to desire to regulate the details of our lives is the strongest proof of love He could give…and to let us know just how to live and walk so as perfectly to please Him seems almost too good to be true.

Hannah W. Smith, *The Christian's Secret to a Happy Life* [3]

THE PRAY METHOD

Prepare. Prepare to understand the text by setting the background. On this day we will look at the context of the passage we are studying. The author, the audience, the setting, and themes of the book. We will always keep the big picture in mind. You will answer: *who? what? where? when?*

Read. On the second day, we will focus on reading. We will start to notice key words and phrases. We will use this day to write the text. When we physically write out the words of Scripture for ourselves, we slow down and read it more slowly. This practice will help us begin to see details.

A Little Deeper. This is the day we will dig deeper into the text. We will study smaller phrases and words in the text. We will look in other passages of Scripture. We will use a dictionary and thesaurus to help us. We will study Scripture with Scripture. Reading God's Word in context and looking at cross references is the best tool for figuring out what a word or phrase means.

Your Turn. After you look at what the passage *says*, it is your turn to look at the passage and determine what it *means*. Put the pieces of the first two days together to form what you think the passage means. Now you will answer the question, why. It is important you still do not consult a commentary. Try to figure out the purpose of the verses before looking at what others have to say.

Conclusion: The very last step in studying the Bible is application. We tend to want to skip ahead to apply God's truth to our lives right away. If you do the hard work of the first few days, the application section will not only be easier to determine, it will be focused on what the text says, not on what you think or believe. You will also be encouraged to find a trusted commentary to use as well.

Chapter 1

Jesus Loves Me, This I Know

Let me tell you a story of a father and a son. A father's son ran away.
Before he ran, he made sure to insult; maybe he yelled. He left in
anger and with a sense of entitlement. He left on his own and by
his own choice. No matter what caused the young man to turn his
back on his father, he did. I suspect it had something to do with a void—a
deep sense of longing in his heart for something…something more than
he had. And he began trying to fill that emptiness. Maybe he tried friends.
Or food. Or fun.

However he did it, he found himself emptier than before and in a
place of disgust and dishonor. In the middle of a pig pen, eating garbage,
he reached the end of his destitution. So the son began to walk home.
Only a spark of hope and a dash of humility kept his feet moving forward.
Maybe his heart practiced the speech. Maybe his lips quivered in fear and
hurt. His eyes surely watered as he expected the justifiable rejection waiting at the end of the road. Humility was his companion during the walk
home.

Before the son could reach the utter place of humiliation, the father
ran to him. Every day the father had been watching for him. Never giving
up hope. Never losing an ounce of love for his wayward son. The father
didn't care about the past. The father cared only that his son had returned.
The father ran up and hugged his son. The son who had shunned him, hated him, insulted him, and left him—this was the son the father embraced.
(Taken from Luke 15:11–32)

Daily living begins here…with love. Daily living is in the truth of this old song I sing to my little ones every night.

Jesus loves me.

This I know,

For the Bible tells me so.

Yes, Jesus loves me.

Jesus asks us to abide in this love. This week we will be reading 1 John. We will discover how abiding in God's love is not just something we do once, and its complete. Abiding is a constant motion.

Don't let the simplicity of love hinder you from the grandeur of it. Yes, Jesus' love for you is simple and unconditional, but it is also deep—so deep we will never reach the bottom. Let's say like Paul:

For I am sure that neither death nor life, nor angels nor rulers, nor things present nor things to come, nor powers, nor height nor depth, nor anything else in all creation, will be able to separate us from the love of God in Christ Jesus our Lord.

Romans 8:38–39

Read it again. NOTHING can separate you. Not the ordinary moments of your life. Not the mundane or the melancholy waiting to greet you each morning. Not your past mistakes. Not the unknown future. The strength, the courage, the hope, and the grace waiting for each day are rooted in love. Not just any love but the love of the Father. Let's start with love.

My oldest son adores me. He will still hug and kiss me, even at eight years old. I love it. I hope he will always write me love notes and whisper his affection to me. He most often offers these words of tenderness when he is in trouble or avoiding a job. I ask him to unload the dishwasher or to let the dog outside. He comes up to wrap his arms around me. I love his desire to be close to me—but not at that moment. What I want in that moment is obedience. I tell him frequently, "Son, if you want to show your love to me, obey me."

A little stab of guilt echoes in my own heart as I utter these words. I hear my Father say the same thing to me: "Sarah, if you want to show me your love and devotion, obey my commandments." The beauty of our relationship—between me and my son—is that my love is not based on his performance. I began loving him as a helpless baby, unconditionally. His obedience is not a reflection of how much I love him. Even in my weakest human efforts, I can love my son even when he disobeys. I will always choose him.

God does the same. One of the ways we can show our love back to God is to obey. When we realize how much God loves us, we are free to love others. And loving on a daily basis is the true test of faith and reliance on God. As we study 1 John together, let's open our hearts to what God would teach about daily love.

Day 1 – Prepare

Read I John. Answer the following questions. You might have to look in a study Bible or an online source for these questions. You can read an introduction to I John here (https://bible.org/seriespage/introduction-1-john).

Optional Task: Print off a copy of the entire text. (www.biblestudytools.com/esv/).

Who wrote 1 John?

When was it written? To whom?

In what style was it written?

Do any words/phrases stand out?

Why do you think John wrote his letter?

- -

I John was written by the apostle John. Some refer to him as the "Beloved Apostle." One of Christ's closest companions. Most believe John wrote the letter to a variety of churches during his exile on the island of Patmos. It was a place of punishment for his belief in Jesus as Christ. John writes to the believers to encourage them to stand firm in the things they believe. His themes include the deity of Christ, the love of God, and forgiveness of sin. We will focus our efforts this week on I John 3:11-4:21. However, to get a good feel of the entire book, read all of I John today.

Work on memorizing *John 15:9-10 - As the Father has loved me, so have I loved you. Abide in my love. If you keep my commandments, you will abide in my love, just as I have kept my Father's commandments and abide in his love.* Write it on a card.

Write out a prayer to God, giving thanks for His incredible Word.

_____

_____

_____

_____

_____

Day 2 – Read

Read I John 3:11-4:21. Answer the following question. Try to answer these questions without looking in a commentary. Optional Task: Read the verses in at least two different translations.

The follow words are repeated in this passage:
TRUTH - LOVE - SPIRIT - ABIDE

Look up each word and write out a definition from a dictionary and a thesaurus.

TRUTH

LOVE

SPIRIT

ABIDE

Write a paraphrase (in your own words) of 1 John 3:11-4:21. Be brief. Make bullet points or just write one-two sentences. Ask yourself, what is the author trying to say?

What additional words stand out for you today?

Work on memorizing *John 15:9-10 - As the Father has loved me, so have I loved you. Abide in my love. If you keep my commandments, you will abide in my love, just as I have kept my Father's commandments and abide in his love.* Write it out below:

_____

_____

_____

Finish this prayer: Lord, I praise you for Your love...

_____

_____

_____

_____

Day 3 – A Little Deeper

Read I John 3:11-4:21 again. Answer the following questions. Try to answer these questions without looking in a commentary. Optional Task: Listen to the passage or the entire book of I John being read aloud. (http://www.biblestudytools.com/audio-bible/)

The next few verses are called *cross references*. They are just verses written by the same author (John) in a separate part of the Bible (the Gospel of John). Write any observations you have about these verses and how they might relate to I John 3:11-4:21.

TRUTH: John 1:14 and John 8:32

LOVE: John 3:16 and John 14:21-24

SPIRIT: John 4:23 and John 16:13

ABIDE: John 8:31 and John 15:1-7

Work on memorizing *John 15:9-10 - As the Father has loved me, so have I loved you. Abide in my love. If you keep my commandments, you will abide in my love, just as I have kept my Father's commandments and abide in his love.* Rewrite the verse in your own words:

_____

_____

_____

_____

Lord, we praise you for your love for us. We give you thanks for your Spirit who indwells our hearts. We pray we will abide more deeply in You today. Amen.

Day 4 – Your Turn

Read I John 3:11-4:21 again. Answer the following questions. Try to answer these questions without looking in a commentary. Optional Task: Read the entire book of I John again.

Look up the following passages on love and make notes.

Psalm 136

Proverbs 3:3

I Corinthians 13:1-13

John 15:9-10

What do all of these ideas have to do with daily love?

How do you describe God's love for you?

· ·

How is His love supposed to be evident in your daily life?

Work on memorizing *John 15:9-10 - As the Father has loved me, so have I loved you. Abide in my love. If you keep my commandments, you will abide in my love, just as I have kept my Father's commandments and abide in his love.* Write it out below (maybe in a different translation):

_____

_____

_____

_____

Finish this prayer: Lord, I praise you for Your Spirit and Truth...

_____

_____

_____

Day 5 – Conclusion

Read I John 3:11-4:21 again. Answer the following questions.

What aspect of God's character has been revealed in the text?

How is this character trait illustrated?

How does understanding that characteristic of God change the way you should think and act?

How can I better live in daily love based on truths from I John 3:11-4:21?

Try to write *John 15:9-10* from memory!

_____

_____

_____

_____

_____

_____

_____

_____

Write your prayer to God, thanking Him for His love for you...

_____

_____

_____

_____

_____

Chapter 2
Coffee Cups of Grace

"If I do my duty, not for duty's sake, but because I believe God is engineering my circumstances, then at the very point of my obedience the whole suburb grace of God is mine through Atonement."

– Oswald Chambers, My Utmost for His Highest [5]

I think the way you like your coffee says something about you. Black coffee drinkers have been drinking since they were born. A little bit of sugar and creamer people are breakfast coffee drinkers. Lots of creamer with some coffee are the newbies. I'm a newbie. I didn't start drinking coffee until my second son was born. Something about having a two-year-old who wakes up before the birds and a newborn who didn't sleep through the night until he was nine months old required coffee. Although that was five years ago, I still take my coffee with lots of creamer.

I used to think of grace as a huge, vast ocean, something big and grand, never ending. Or maybe grace was like a well that would never run dry. The grace of God seemed measureless, and it was hard for me to grasp the idea of grace on a daily basis. But what if we looked at grace as more like a cup of coffee?

I don't make enough coffee for my entire life every day. I don't even make enough coffee for the whole week on Monday morning. On Monday morning, I make enough coffee for Monday. Just Monday. Sometimes I'll make a new pot for the afternoon as well. Not just because coffee a week old would taste a little stale, but because I don't need to. I trust that tomorrow I can wake up and my coffee can be made, just a few cups at a time.

The path through life is full of unknowns, so I always feared there wouldn't be enough grace for the unknowns. I knew I had grace for the trials I had once faced or the grace to live in today, but what about tomorrow? Suddenly, I realized grace wasn't an ocean. I had enough grace just for today. And if I focus on the big picture of grace—enough grace to last a lifetime—I have the tendency to be overwhelmed by the sheer volume of the idea of grace.

I don't think God gives us grace in big, huge gallon jugs. God gives us coffee cups of grace. Just enough grace for today. Maybe enough grace for a moment. I trust my coffee pot, water, and coffee will be available every morning, ready for me. I can count on it. Why do I doubt that the God of the universe and the Savior of my soul is able to provide enough grace for today?

Enough grace for all of the unknowns. Enough grace for the tantrums waiting for me in the afternoon. Enough grace for sick babies at 2 a.m. Enough grace for when my husband is running late from work. Enough grace to handle dinner alone. Enough grace to encourage instead of discourage when my son comes up with a crazy idea. Enough grace to answer a friend who is struggling with fear. Enough grace to combat the lies whispering in my heart.

Grace for our sins, for the storm, for the moment, and especially for today. Yes, it is by grace we are saved, but it is through grace we live. Grace means the favor of God. Grace is not some mystical object, feeling, or state of being. Grace is found in doing one thing: obedience. Grace and obedience work together.

It is so interesting, the relationship between grace and obedience. They coexist despite the paradox. They are so closely tied together that I imagine them like a piece of rope. The big, huge, yacht-like rope. The rope on a big boat holds the boat to the dock and keeps the vessel from floating away. Grace and obedience are separate things but work together.

The source of grace may seem simple, but do we grasp the depths of it? Yes, Jesus is our source, but do we see all He is to us? Do we see all He could be if we would let Him? Living in daily grace begins with a relationship. I cannot take it for granted you know Jesus personally, so I cannot go further in this study unless I can share with you first about Jesus. Maybe you know *about* Jesus. Maybe you prayed a prayer or went forward in a church once a long time ago.

Christ came to Earth in the form of a baby. We know He was more than just human (John 1:1). He was also divine, God in the flesh. As He lived a perfect life, meeting all of the requirements of God's law, He showed us how to walk through life. His life is a reflection of how our lives should be. To fulfill all of God's law, a sacrifice had to be made. A blood sacrifice was required (Deut. 12:27) for forgiveness of sins. We are required to pay the price for sin, and the price is death (Romans 6:23). Jesus paid that ransom for us. He died for our sins—once and for all. Jesus didn't want to come to just show us how to live. He came to die. For you. And for me. You see, we didn't need an example; we needed a Savior.

If you have never given your life to Him, turn your eyes upon Him today. Confess your sins. Believe He died and rose again for your sins. Accept the free gift of grace today!

Grab your cup of coffee (or tea), and take a big sip of it. Imagine it as grace. Enough. Lean into His arms, and let's discover grace for today.

Oh God of grace, fill my cup for today. Let me not worry about
the future and if there will be enough. I pray you will give me
just enough grace for today. Amen.

Day 1 – Prepare

Letters today fly from screen to screen. No longer are we physically passing on news via the snail-mail method. There is something we lose when we give up physical letter writing. A piece of someone is sent with the letter when it is mailed. Imagine holding a letter from Paul, the Apostle! In the New Testament, many of the books we read were actual letters. Held and handed over physically. Today's passage comes from the letter to Ephesus. Paul wrote to the Christians there to encourage them in their faith. He desires to paint a picture of the Gospel for them.

> Read Ephesians 2 and answer the following questions. Optional Task: Print off a copy of the entire text for this week. (Ephesians 2) (www.biblestudytools.com/esv/).

Who wrote this passage? When was it written? To whom? In what style was it written? You might also read Ephesians 1:1-2 or check in a study Bible's introduction to the book.

Do you see any words repeated? Write them down.

Write a ***brief*** paraphrase, as you understand the passage today. Just one or two sentences to sum up the chapter.

Start memorizing: *Ephesians 2:8 - "For by grace you have been saved through faith."*

Let's write it out today!

_____

_____

_____

_____

Write out a prayer to God thanking Him for His salvation and grace to you.

_____

_____

_____

_____

Day 2 – Read

Read Ephesians 1-4. As you read through the first part of this letter, remember it was originally written to be read out loud to a church. Before we begin searching for answers, let's remember to keep the big picture in mind. After you have read the four chapters, look at Ephesians 2:1-6 again. Circle the words you think are important. Make notes on this page or your printed text. Highlight or circle the big ideas, especially related to salvation, grace, and so on. Did you see any phrases you don't understand? Any confusing words? Make a note to look up these phrases later.

Write out Ephesians 2:1-6. Optional Task: Read Ephesians 2 in a different translation.

_____

_____

_____

_____

_____

_____

_____

_____

_____

_____

_____

_____

_____

_____

_____

Write a prayer of reflection after finishing writing the text.

_____

_____

_____

_____

Continue memorizing: *Ephesians 2:8 - "For by grace you have been saved through faith."*

Write it on a card to hang somewhere in your home.

Day 3 – A Little Deeper

> Look up *grace*. Write down the definitions you find in both a dictionary **and** a thesaurus.

When we use other passages to help explain or further our understanding of a certain passage, **we are studying the Bible *with* the Bible!**

GRACE

As the letter to Ephesians continues, Paul begins to get practical. He says in the first part of the letter, *look at what grace did for you!* In the second part, he says, *look at what you should do because of grace!* What does Paul say about grace in Ephesians 4:1-7?

In 1 and 2 Corinthians Paul is writing to believers to help them remember the truths they had been taught. Many false teachers were popping up in the church, causing divisions. Persecution was heavy on their hearts as well. Paul concludes his letter to the church in Corinth by reminding them of all they had because of Christ and grace.

Read 2 Corinthians 2:8-10. What does Paul say about grace?

. . . .

How many times do you wake up and feel you aren't enough for that day? Many times I wake up feeling, *"I've got this day!"* But there are just as many days I lay in bed and want to cover my head again. The demands of the day seem too big. Too much for me. The strength of Christ is rooted in grace. As we begin to understand the idea of grace through Ephesians 2, we will see how we have just enough (a coffee cup) for today.

Continue memorizing: *Ephesians 2:8 - "For by grace you have been saved through faith."* Say the verse aloud three times.

O Lord, I praise you for your word! Today help me to remember your grace is indeed enough for today. I can rest in knowing my strength is in YOU, not in myself. It is ok that I am weak today. For your grace is enough. Amen.

Optional Task: Compare and Contrast Life BEFORE Grace and AFTER Grace

Before Salvation - Before Grace	After Salvation - After Grace
Ephesians 2:1-3	Ephesians 2:4-10
Ephesians 2:11-12	Ephesians 2:13-14, 19-22

Day 4 – Your Turn

In Ephesians 2, what does Paul say about...

our salvation? Who is the power, author, and authority behind our salvation?

grace? What does grace look like, if you were to try to explain it?

What does Paul say about walking in Eph. 2:10? Read Ephesians 4:1-7. How do we "walk in grace"?

Write a paraphrase of Ephesians 2. What was Paul trying to tell the church about grace? About salvation? About being "one" in Christ?

Continue memorizing: *Ephesians 2:8 - "For by grace you have been saved through faith."*

Write a paraphrase of the verse:

_____

_____

_____

_____

_____

_____

_____

_____

Dear Jesus, today I want to walk in grace. Help me to live today in a manner worthy of my calling. With your grace filling me every morning, I can pour myself out for others. I can walk in humility and gentleness because your grace is enough for today. Amen.

Optional Task: Write out Ephesians 4:1-7 and reflect on God's calling for you to walk in grace. (see next page)

Write out Ephesians 4:1-7

Write a prayer of reflection after finishing writing the text.

Day 5 – Conclusion

The purpose for Bible study isn't necessarily to *feel better about ourselves*. It is about discovering who God is in the pages of Scripture. When we discover who God is, we can also find comfort and peace. But we also realize areas where we need to change. The questions today are for your reflection and application. You can consult a trusted commentary and compare your notes with the author's notes. What additional truths did you find? Did the commentary answer some of your questions? How?

What aspect of God's character has been revealed in the text?

How is this character trait illustrated?

How does understanding this characteristic of God change the way you should think and act?

How can I better live in daily grace based on truths from Ephesians?

How is knowing that Christ paid it all a strength for me today?

What truth about God do I need to rest in today?

Try to write *Ephesians 2:8* from memory!

_____

_____

_____

Write your prayer to God, thanking Him for His grace...

_____

_____

_____

Chapter 3
Just Take a Nap

"Please take a nap," I whispered to my three and half year old, rubbing her back. She stubbornly crossed her arms while sitting up in bed. Stuffed animals lined the wall, and her brow was furrowed. The special pink blanket and purple pillow were with her. The sounds of waves from the sound machine played softly. It was an hour since nap time had started. The boys were quiet in the basement. The youngest was snoring loudly in the next room.

I had been upstairs to put the willful toddler back into bed four times. The afternoon sun shone through the window. Outside, the green trees blew in the breeze, promising a beautiful day. I laid her back down and covered her up.

"One more book!" she pleaded.

"No," I replied.

"One more song!" she begged.

"No, it is nap time."

Tears rolled down her cheeks as she screamed, "I don't want to take a nap time!"

Nap time is usually my quiet time and my favorite time of the day. I can finally breathe. I can let my shoulders relax just a little. I do my best never to schedule any appointments during nap time. Don't mess with nap time. I love my time of rest. It is sometimes short and interrupted, but it doesn't matter what I get to do as long as I do it alone. Most days my stubborn three-year-old will lay down, but sometimes she interrupts my rest time. As she fights rest time, I see a reflection of myself.

I'm always wanting rest in my life, but it seems like I fight it. Don't we all sometimes resist the rest offered to us? We demand to keep busy. There is just too much to do. We have too many things on our plates. Business is the archenemy to rest. Most of my time is stolen not by resting but by doing work. Valuable work. And a lot of waiting would seem to be about keeping busy. Like Mary at the feet of Jesus, choosing time to be with Christ is the better choice. The better choice is to rest.

A life lived in the daily is a life with pockets of rest. On days filled with busy toddlers and babies who won't sleep through the night, I wish (only secretly) I might break my leg. I imagine the doctors would fill me with pain meds and then set me on my bed to rest for weeks on end. I just want to sleep! Taking care of little people and a house along with serving at church wears me down. Do you ever have days when you think, "I'll get some rest today!" Only to find yourself interrupted over and over again? On those days, my husband comes home from work to a very frazzled wife and momma. It is harder to keep my composure when I expected to get rest and then didn't.

No matter how often we fight the urge to rest, we need to give in to it—daily. As my daughter struggled to get out of my arms during her nap, I held her. I gave her the warning of a punishment if she got out of bed again. My two older boys were closer to five years old before they were outgrowing their naps. Someone told me once that they believed strong-willed children didn't need as much sleep. I believe it. Some days she and I go around and around in the nap-time battle. Some days she finally gives in to her body's need for sleep. Sometimes I give up and let her stay up to watch a show on TV.

There is no magic formula for us to find rest in our lives. I can only tell you what I tell her: "Stop fighting it." Give in and make time to rest.

Mommy, I need…

More to drink…more cereal…a napkin…more syrup, ketchup, ranch dressing…

At every meal, I'm the waitress, bringing refills and serving my little people. It's okay. Breakfast and lunch are usually eaten after (sometimes before) they eat, so I walk back and forth from the table to the refrigerator. It's okay. I realize it is only a season. Soon enough, they will be old enough to refill their own glasses. Until then, I can serve. I can refill them. Again. And again. Their need to be filled is a reflection of my own heart.

It is scary to be empty. It is exhausting to wake up tired. When I wake up from the sound of footsteps and voices echoing in the hallway, I just want to pull the covers over my head. It is a little frightening to feel the void and know in my heart I can never fill myself. I don't have enough to give them all they need. It is scary to be hollow and discover the empty spaces in our hearts.

With a house full of kids and a husband with 12-hour shifts, I drink my coffee while inside I feel so…empty. *"For I am already being poured out as a drink offering…"* (2 Tim. 4:6–8). Poured out. Emptied. Paul looked into his soul and emptied it all, on purpose. His cup was never full. He wasn't just empty but deliberate about becoming empty. Paul choose the life of sacrifice by offering his life, his relationships, his work, and his calling on the altar to God. He did it for people and the gospel. He was busy doing the best work, not busy work.

Every time I pour the milk and snap the lid back on, the little hands reaching for me mean I am being emptied, and in the sacrifice of myself, I find Him right beside me, filling me again. And again. Jesus is the Living Water. I can let the cool streams wash over my daily life again and again. I gladly offer myself to those around me. For in emptiness, I find myself full, in Christ.

Rest is the best way to fill our hearts. Drawing away from the crowds is something even Jesus needed to do. Yet we need to be wise about how we rest. Our seasons of life will ebb and flow, never staying the same. The way we rest now will not be how we rest in six months, two years, or ten years from now. We must learn to cultivate a heart of rest.

What is the secret? Be wholly occupied with Jesus. Sink the roots of your being in faith and love and obedience deep down into Him. Come away out of every other place to abide here. Give up everything for the inconceivable privilege of being a branch on earth of the glorified Son of God in Heaven. Let Christ be first. Let Christ be all. **Do not be occupied with the abiding—be occupied with Christ.** *He will hold you, He will keep you abiding in Him. He will abide in you. – Andrew Murray* [7]

Oh Christ, be close to me today. Let me find a few minutes for prayer and rest. Let me be intentional about seeking you out, knowing you will fill my cup again and again. Amen.

Day 1 – Prepare

Read Mark 1:1. Where does Mark start in Jesus' life? Jesus' birth? Childhood? Adulthood?

Who wrote the book of Mark? this passage?

What do you think the author's purpose or reason for writing might have been?

Mark's gospel was written as a very fast paced narrative. Mark doesn't give any type of introduction. He begins with a story about John the Baptist and Jesus. What story does Mark begin with in Mark 1:9?

Mark's focus, many believe, was written for non-Jewish readers. Many believe Peter helped Mark to write the gospel. The Jewish customs and rituals are explained throughout Mark, and Jesus is portrayed as more of a Messiah for all nations, not just a Jewish Messiah. Many of the miracles and accounts focus around Jesus' interactions with non-Jewish people. In Mark's gospel we see Jesus as the perfect example of a servant. Through Jesus' acts of compassion, Mark demonstrates Jesus' desire to save us from our sins. Read Mark 1:15. What was Jesus' message?

Read Mark 6:7-52 to familiarize yourself with the passage. What can you tell me about this passage? Write a paraphrase (in your own words) the passage.

Start memorizing: *Mark 6:31 - "And he [Jesus] said to them [the disciples], 'Come away by yourselves to a desolate place and rest a while"* Let's write it out today!

_____   _____

_____

_____

_____

_____

Write out a prayer to God asking His word to encourage your heart today.

_____

_____

_____

_____

_____

Day 2 – Read

Today, let's read the passage again (Mark 6:7-52). This time write the events in order.

What happened in Mark 6:7-14?

What happened in Mark 6:14-29?

What happened in Mark 6:30-44?

What happened in Mark 6:45-52?

It might seem these passages have several different stories strung together, with no correlation. Stick with me! You will be amazed by the connection by the end of the week. Today, let's deal with the first two sections. In verses 7-14 Jesus is sending out His disciples. Remember from yesterday, Mark's emphasis is Jesus' message of healing, leading to repentance, leading to forgiveness and salvation. Jesus wanted to spread that gospel throughout the land, so He gave the disciples special instructions and sent them out. What did the disciples do? Mark 6:12-13.

Remember their hard work and ministry for tomorrow's lesson. For now, let's briefly cover the parenthetical passage of Mark 6:14-29. It is the record of John the Baptist's death. Remember John the Baptist from day one. He baptized Jesus, but he was also the prophet who proclaimed Jesus' coming. Not only that, John was Jesus' cousin (see Luke 1). The death of His cousin surely touched Jesus' heart. Let's keep that in mind when we study tomorrow what Jesus wants to do next.

Continue memorizing *Mark 6:31 - "And he [Jesus] said to them [the disciples], 'Come away by yourselves to a desolate place and rest a while'"*

Write it on a card to hang somewhere in your house.

───────────────────❧───────────────────

Dear Lord, I praise you for the opportunity to serve others.
I understand I need to take time to rest, but let me not be
discouraged when my rest time is interrupted. Teach me
compassion. Amen.

───────────────────❧───────────────────

Day 3 – A Little Deeper

Refresh your memory from yesterday (Mark 6:12-13)

What did Jesus send the disciples out to do? What happened when they went out?

What did they want to do when they returned?

Read Mark 6:30-32. Instead of having them report to Him, Jesus asked the disciples to do what?

On their way to find rest and pray, what happens? Read Mark 6:33-44. Retell the story in just a few sentences.

Look up the word "compassion" using (https://www.biblegateway.com). What other verses have that word in them?

How does the dictionary define "compassion"? What other words are found in the thesaurus for "compassion"?

What struck me the most about this passage is Jesus wasn't even fazed by the crowd. He wasn't bothered or irritated even though they were interrupting His time of rest. His disciples were tired. He was tired; they had spent so much energy on serving and ministry and preaching the gospel, only to be interrupted. Do we find ourselves in the same situation, every day? My time of rest is always interrupted time, but can I look on the people around me with eyes as Jesus - eyes full of compassion for them? Write out a time you were interrupted. How did you respond?

How can you respond next time more like Jesus?

Jesus used the interruption to minister. He not only provided their physical needs, but also saw their spiritual needs. Sometimes rest is interrupted, and that's ok. Sometimes physical needs need to be met, sometimes spiritual needs. But Jesus didn't let the crowd take His entire day. Tomorrow we will see if He did indeed get to rest.

Dear Jesus, today I want to walk in rest. But my rest is always interrupted. Let me see with eyes of compassion those around me. Let me trust you in the middle of ministry moments. Let me believe rest is coming. Amen.

Continue memorizing *Mark 6:31 - "And he [Jesus] said to them [the disciples], 'Come away by yourselves to a desolate place and rest a while'"* Say the verse aloud three times.

Day 4 – Your Turn

Read Mark 6:45-46. What did Jesus finally get to do? What were the disciples doing?

What happened in Mark 6:47-52? Rewrite the events in the story.

Read Matthew 8:23-27 and Luke 8:22-25. Do you think these are the same stories? How are they different? Alike?

Why do you think Mark included this story with the feeding of the five thousand?

The men had just finished two huge ministry opportunities. The first was being sent out and preaching and healing. The second was the amazing miracle on the hillside. After both accounts, the disciples went back to work. They didn't take time to rest. Do you think there is a correlation? Jesus spent time in prayer, but did the disciples?

What conclusions can you draw about fear, faith, rest, and ministry?

Continue memorizing: *Mark 6:31 - "And he [Jesus] said to them [the disciples], 'Come away by yourselves to a desolate place and rest a while'"* Write a paraphrase of the verse:

_____

_____

_____

_____

Optional Task: Make a list of what a commentary said vs. what you wrote about Mark 6 to share with the group.

Day 5 – Conclusion

The purpose for Bible study isn't necessarily to *feel better about ourselves*. It is about discovering who God is in the pages of Scripture. When we discover who God is, we can also find comfort and peace. But we also realize areas where we need to change. The questions today are for your reflection and application.

What aspect of God's character has been revealed in the text?

How is this character trait illustrated?

How does understanding this characteristic of God change the way you should think and act?

How can I better live in daily rest based on truths from Mark?

Did Jesus forget to rest? What did He do during His time of rest? (Mark 6:46).

Prayer doesn't have to be all we do during our times of rest. Today, make a list of all of the things you would like to do if you had time to rest. Then circle one you can do today. Then DO IT! We can't all take spa days every day, but like Mary and Martha, we can choose the better choice. Read Matthew 11:28-30. What type of "burden" does Jesus lay on us? How can this give us comfort today?

What truth about God do I need rest in today?

Try to write *Mark 6:31* from memory!

_____

_____

_____

_____

_____

Write your prayer to God, thanking Him for giving you daily rest...

_____

_____

_____

_____

_____

_____

_____

_____

_____

_____

My List of Restful Activities:

_____

_____

_____

_____

_____

Chapter 4

Melt the Ice

My children loved this simple activity I found on Pinterest. I took a bucket, about twelve inches long and six inches deep, filled it with water, and then placed a few toys in the water. After letting it freeze overnight, I let them take the block of ice outside on our slanted driveway. It took them almost an hour to melt the ice and chip away at the toys locked inside.

I think about joy as the toys inside that block of ice. Sometimes I think joy is stuck inside of me, frozen and inaccessible because of my heart. My heart is full of worry and anxiety. No matter how hard I try to chip away at the anxiety and fear, no amount of effort on my part breaks joy free. I try to not be anxious for anything…but then something comes up and I'm anxious again.

When it comes to joy, I struggle. Maybe the hardest lesson I've learned through daily living is how to find joy. I think I still have more to learn. Joy can seem so elusive, like trying to hold on to a piece of ice. It is just too slippery and cold.

It is frustrating for me to hear phrases like:

Choose Joy.

Fight for Joy.

Let Go and Find Joy.

I've tried it. I've mentally tried to will myself to have joy. I've fought for joy, especially during the waiting of the adoption. I've let go, and joy didn't come. In fact, when I let go of trying for joy, I felt even more like a failure. I was missing something—and I still didn't have joy. I'm not saying I never smiled or laughed. Happiness is very much a part of my reality—but the deep feeling of joyful satisfaction never seemed to fit me. I felt I could never get ahold of it.

Last summer as my children chipped away at the ice, I sat in the cool shade of the garage just watching them. I finally told them the secret: wait and let the ice melt. Use your hands to melt the ice. They giggled with enthusiasm as the water dripped down the driveway and into the garage where I was sitting. It was working. Their efforts and the sun's efforts worked together to melt the ice. When the first toy was extracted, a new determination took over! They threw away their chipping tools and used the secret to melting ice: the sun.

Just as my children needed the sun, I also must rely on the Son. As Jesus spoke to His disciples on the night before His death, He spoke about abiding, the Holy Spirit, and joy. All three are so closely tied together that without one, we cannot have the others. Jesus promises us fruit when we abide in Him. And what does Paul say is a fruit of the Spirit? Joy. Joy is a fruit of abiding.

Join me as we discover how God can thaw the joy from our hearts daily. It isn't about finding joy once. It is about living in joy every day. And the secret isn't a secret! It's in the abiding. Let's study John 16 together to find the joy God has for us.

All of the houses in our neighborhood are built on the side of a hill. My friend from another part of the state was shocked at the curvy roads winding in and out, up and down, under and over the green hills. In the winter, the view behind our house is full of branches and trees and sometimes snow. When we first walked into our house, our eyes were immediately drawn to the view in the back. Trees, bushes, and branches give the illusion of being in the middle of the woods. In fact, we are only a stone's throw away from several neighbors.

Right outside my kitchen window three huge trees tower above the rest of the shrubbery. I look at these trees every day, no matter the season, and they are always green. They are not evergreen trees. They are trees covered in vines. When I think about the "true vine" mentioned in John 15, I sometimes think about these green vines.

I love Cynthia Heald's definition of abiding:

"Abiding in Christ is deciding to let Christ be our Source, surrounding our life for His life, seeking His kingdom and His righteousness, trusting Him to provide all that we need. It is choosing each day to spend time with Him."

How do we do that? Right now. You are doing it! You may think that joy is really far away right now. Circumstances and emotions will tell you otherwise, but true abiding leads to joy. I've found that when we get pushed into the deep end and don't know how to swim, joy will find us in unexpected places. It isn't our job to find joy. It is our job to abide. Let's study the visual of the true vine to explore joy.

I come to the garden alone
While the dew is still on the roses
And the voice I hear falling on my ear
The Son of God discloses.

And He walks with me, and He talks with me,
And He tells me I am His own;
And the joy we share as we tarry there,
None other has ever known.

– C. Austin Miles [9]

Come to the garden where the vine rests. He is calling you to make your home in Him. To seek Him first. To put Him first in your life. When He is first, your joy will come. As we put Christ first, joy will come each day.

Dear Father, meet me here in the garden today. Walk with me,
restoring joy, your joy, in my life. I pray you will help me rejoice,
no matter if it is a season of storms or sunshine. Amen.

Day 1 – Prepare

Many have described the Gospel of John as a deep pool where elephants could wade, but shallow enough for children to play. John's message of Jesus is so incredibly deep, scholars are still plummeting the depths. Yet, as we will learn this week, you don't need a doctorate degree to understand the profound truths in these verses. First, let's get some context.

> Who wrote John? Take a look in your study Bible or (https:// bible.org/seriespage/introduction-john) to find out what you can about John.

Read John 13:1. What time of the year was it? What was going to happen in the next few days?

Jesus was getting ready to die, and before He left, He wanted to impart some important truths to the disciples. John 14-16 record Jesus' words to His apostles during the last supper. In chapter fourteen, Jesus talks about the only way to see the Father. He calls Himself the Way, the Truth, and the Life. In chapter fifteen, what does Jesus call Himself (John 15:1)?

What does Jesus call us? What are we asked to do? (John 15:5).

Joy will be discussed in chapter sixteen, but we cannot miss the message of chapter fifteen. What is the theme of John 15?

What does "abiding" have to do with joy?

Start memorizing *John 16:24 - "Ask, and you will receive, that your joy may be full."* Let's write it out today!

_____

_____

_____

_____

_____

_____

Write out a prayer asking God to help you abide in Him today.

_____

_____

_____

Day 2 – Read

Read John 16:1-4 and John 16:33. Why did Jesus say these words to His disciples?

Who is mentioned in verses 7-15?

What will the Spirit do according to verses 12-15?

What is the Spirit's ultimate goal? See John 16:14.

The word "trinity" is never mentioned in the Bible, but does this passage give evident of it? How?

Write out John 16:33.

_____

_____

_____

Tomorrow we will look at how Jesus' words on sorrow and joy can give us unshakeable peace. For now, let's give thanks for the Spirit's work in our lives.

Continue memorizing *John 16:24 - "Ask, and you will receive, that your joy may be full."* Write it on a card to hang somewhere in your house.

Write out a prayer to God thanking Him for the person of the Holy Spirit.

_____

_____

_____

_____

_____

_____

Day 3 – A Little Deeper

Read John 16:20-24. What illustration does Jesus use to describe sorrow and joy?

If you described sorrow transforming to joy, what illustration would you use?

Compare and contrast JOY and SORROW. Look in a dictionary AND a thesaurus.

Read these passages on joy. What do you find?

1. Galatians 5:22

2. I Thessalonians 1:6

3. James 1:2-3

Dear Jesus, today I want to walk in joy. I understand joy and sorrow will fill this day. Maybe today holds more sorrow than joy, but I will praise you still. Joy isn't something I can muster up, but it is something I find when I abide in you. Amen.

Continue memorizing *John 16:24 - "Ask, and you will receive, that your joy may be full."* Say the verse aloud three times.

Day 4 – Your Turn

Read John 16:16-24 again. What two words did we study yesterday?

How are those two words related to the Holy Spirit, according to John 16?

Read John 15:9-11. What does abiding in God's love have to do with joy?

What is the benefit of sorrow when it comes to finding joy?

What do you think the purpose of John 15-16 was? What is Jesus' conclusion about suffering and joy?

. . . .

Write down five things you can find joy in for today.

1.

2.

3.

4.

5.

. . . .

Continue memorizing: *John 16:24 - "Ask, and you will receive, that your joy may be full."* Write a paraphrase of the verse:

_____

_____

_____

_____

Day 5
Conclusion

Read John 15-16:24.

What aspect of the Holy Spirit's character has been revealed in the text?

How is this character trait illustrated?

How does understanding that characteristic of God change the way you should think and act?

Joy feels and comes from different places for different people. Finish the following sentences:

Joy isn't...

Joy is...

How can you better live in daily *joy* based on truths from John 15-16?

Try to write *John 16:24* from memory!

_____

_____

_____

_____

Write your prayer to God, thanking Him for giving you daily joy.....

_____

_____

_____

_____

_____

_____

Chapter 5

The Secret of Prayer

I sat beside my five-year-old one night in church. He was a little fidgety. I let him wiggle during the service, except for the end. The pastor always opens up the altar on Sunday evenings for a time of prayer. As he struggled to be still, I whispered to him, "Right now is quiet time. We are going to pray to God. You can too. Ask God to help you with something you are struggling with."

He whispered back, "What are you struggling with, Mommy?"

I blurted out, "Being a good mommy."

His eyes widened as he looked at me, wondering why I would pray such a silly prayer. Maybe in his mind he believed I was already a good mommy. Maybe he didn't understand the guilt mommies feel sometimes. I felt ashamed I had admitted to my little guy one of my fears. For me, it was a simple prayer: to be a good mommy. It was something I had wished for, but did I believe God would answer me? Did I believe God was answering my request even now?

So many times I overlook the simple. I don't even question the little children when they come to the Heavenly Father with requests of sick puppies and tiny cuts on their knees. I don't reprimand their prayers for a good birthday. I accept the simplicity, except in my own prayers. Occasionally, my boys will share a secret. I invite them to take it to God, to ask Him for the help their hearts need to fight their fears. So when I tell them to take it to God, I am really telling myself.

Thankfully, we will always be able to approach God's throne. We are always welcome to come and lay our requests at the mercy seat and find grace. Prayer is required of us and commanded of us, but prayer is more than that. Prayer is an invitation, a way to connect with the entire Trinity.

I love how prayer requires that we ask each of the members of the Trinity to join us in communion. The Holy Spirit carries our prayers to the Father. He even speaks for us when we have no words to whisper. When the hurt is too deep or our thoughts too clouded, the Spirit lifts our needs to the Father. And there He is, waiting.

The Father is always listening. Psalm 116:1–2 says, "I love the LORD, because he has heard my voice and my pleas for mercy. Because he inclined his ear to me, therefore I will call on him as long as I live." God's ear is always turned toward us. He is never distracted. We can pray anytime, no matter the state of our heart.

Then we have the final member of the Trinity. Christ is sitting next to the Father, always making intercession for us. Hebrews 7:25 tells us, "Consequently, he is able to save to the uttermost those who draw near to God through him, since he always lives to make intercession for them." I never thought Hebrews was much of a book on prayer, but I've found so many lessons in this amazing epistle! As we study prayer, we are going to discover the power of prayer in the person of Jesus Christ. What we believe about Jesus is directly related to how we pray.

As we begin, let's start at the end. It was the ninth hour. Jesus, our Savior, hung on the cross. His body was beaten and bruised. The soldiers and crowd mocked Him. Some wept with fear and uncertainty. In the moment of Jesus' death, the earth quaked and the sun drew dark. The very creation mourned its Creator's death. Tucked away in Jerusalem, in the farthest corner of the temple, was a curtain. It separated the holy of holies from all of God's people. It represented how sin separates us from God. Although it was called a veil, it was heavy and thick, impossible to move without the help of several men. In a flash, it tore in two pieces—from top to bottom—not by human hands but by the very hands of God. In the darkest hour, light and hope shined bright.

Everything has changed. We now have access to God. And in this amazing truth, we find God—with open arms and ready to listen and move. The Holy Spirit is, at this moment, whispering your needs to God. Jesus is on his throne, standing in your place and representing you to the

Father. My son taught me that no prayer is too simple, silly, or secret for God. Our prayer life matters. It is through the power of prayer that we find the strength to live today.

Can I tell you a secret? Knowing God is the key to daily prayer. We know about God, but do you know God through a personal relationship? We do need to know about Him. We study His attributes. Just like when I was dating my husband. I learned what he liked, where he liked to go, and what he liked to do. I learned through conversation. As he and I began walking together through life, we got to know each other. Our relationship grew from just knowing about each other to really knowing the depths of each other's hearts.

More than ten years of marriage have taught me you will never stop getting to know someone. And knowing who they really are takes time. It takes time to cultivate a relationship. It takes walking together through the valleys and mountaintops. When we brought home our daughter from China and all of the medical unknowns overwhelmed us, we hung on to each other. We hung on to God. I can read in my Bible that God is faithful, but as we were pushed into the deep end with only God to hang on to, I experienced God's faithfulness. The difference between praying to know about God and praying to know God are two separate things. Prayer is a matter of communication but also of communion.

Prayer is not simply getting things from God...prayer is getting into perfect communion with God.

– Oswald Chambers [11]

If we desire to live daily with God and develop our relationship with Him, prayer is the perfect place to start. Prayer is where we will find love, grace, rest, and joy. Prayer is the avenue God uses, not to get things done but to show Himself. There is no perfect journaling method, acronym, or secret to prayer, only that we must do it. A habit of daily prayer will not happen overnight, but we should not give up trying.

As I was studying Hebrews recently, I began to realize how much of the book was about prayer. I love what this letter offers us who are struggling with prayer. Let's learn how to cultivate a heart of daily prayer.

Oh Father, full of mercy, bring me close to you. May the Spirit guide me to a place of rest in you. In my Spirit, may I find peace and strength for today. My Savior, Jesus, I give you the glory for the ability to approach the throne of grace. Amen.

Day 1 – Prepare

Before we begin, I want to add a quick note. The study of prayer is so often done with isolated verses. Many times we study prayer without reading the context of each verse. I wish we could dive into every single one of these verses and their context. We do not have time in this book, and it would take an entire Bible study to do so. However, I will include a list at the end of day five if you would like to study further about prayer. I have decided to focus our attention on the *Person of Prayer* for this week.

> Do a little research on the book of Hebrews. It is a pretty deep book, but look at your study Bible or https://bible.org/seriespage/introduction-hebrews to answer some of these questions.

Do we know who wrote Hebrews? Who do some people think wrote it? Based on just the title, who was Hebrews written to?

Read Genesis 12:1-3. Who was the "founder" of the Jewish nation?

Read Genesis 12:7 to find out what he did in response to God's call in his life. Read Genesis 14:18. Who is mentioned as a priest of the Most High God?

God ordained the priesthood even before the Jewish nation was a people group. Beginning with Abram (later called Abraham), including this mysterious man, Melchizedek, then it moved into the linage of Aaron, or the Levites. Read Leviticus 29:1-20 and Hebrews 5:1-4. What needed to be done to purify the priests before they could serve God in the temple?

Who is our Priest today? Read Hebrews 4:14-16.

Now read Hebrews 8:5-6. The author of Hebrews is saying look at the former traditions, the previous priests who have interceded for the Jewish people. They are all shadows of what is to come. Jesus is the perfect priest, the reason we can approach God's throne in prayer. As we study these other "shadows" this week, let's keep in mind the reason we can live as confident Christians in our prayer life is through the Person and Priesthood of Jesus!

Start memorizing *Hebrews 10:23 - "Let us hold on to the confession of our hope without wavering, for He who promised is faithful."* Let's write it out today!

_____

_____

_____

_____

Write out a prayer asking God to help you concentrate this week and find the time to study.

_____

_____

_____

_____

Day 2 – Read

Refresh your memory from yesterday and read Genesis 12:7 and Genesis 14:8. Who are the two men who offered sacrifices to God?

Read Exodus 28:1-4. God is talking to Moses. Who does He tell Moses to bring? What does God want to do with this man's family?

Read Hebrews 5:1-4. How would someone become a priest?

Read Hebrews 7:1-10. Write down the names mentioned here. Record anything you know about these men.

What is the point the author is trying to make with mentioning all of these priests? Read Hebrews 7:22-28 and Hebrews 8:1-3.

Write out Hebrews 7:22.

_____

_____

_____

_____

_____

_____

Continue memorizing *Hebrews 10:23 - "Let us hold on to the confession of our hope without wavering, for He who promised is faithful."* Write it on a card to hang somewhere in your house.

Write out a prayer to Jesus thanking Him for being the perfect Priest.

_____

_____

_____

_____

_____

_____

Day 3 – A Little Deeper

> Look up the following references and find out all you can about Melchizedek. Don't be tempted to look in commentaries! Remember to find out what the text says first, then read what other people have say to about it.

Genesis 14:16-18

Psalm 110:3-5

Hebrews 7:1-10

What other names does he have? Was Salam a real place? If so, where and when?

What do you think it means that he had no "mother and father"?
(Hebrews 7:3)

Next we are going to dig deeper into the Old Testament priesthood. Look up the following references and find out all you can about the priesthood.

Malachi 2:7

Numbers 10:1-10

Leviticus 6:8-13

Leviticus 10:8-11

The High Priest was one priest who was chosen to represent the entire nation to God. Once a year, on the Day of Atonement, he would enter the holy of holies and offer a special sacrifice. You can read in Leviticus 16:14–15 about this sacrifice. Hebrews 5:3 says since he was still a sinner, he had to first make a sacrifice for himself then sacrifice for the people. How is Christ even better than this High Priests? Read Hebrews 7:26-28.

Continue memorizing *Hebrews 10:23* - *"Let us hold on to the confession of our hope without wavering, for He who promised is faithful."* Say the verse aloud three times.

Oh Lord God, you are faithful. So faithful to keep your promises.
We know this because of the promise of the priesthood. Help
me live today in confidence knowing you are on the throne,
interceding for me. Amen.

Day 4 – Your Turn

> Now you can look in your study Bible or online to help you answer some of these questions.

Let's look at Melchizedek again. What are the theories can you find on this man?

What is the significance of where Melchizedek lived?

Read Hebrews 5:1-10. What is the significance and correlation concerning Melchizedek and Christ?

Most scholars agree on a couple of points when we compare Melchizedek to Christ. One of the biggest connections is the idea of the eternal priesthood. Christ is forever going to be our priest, interceding for us throughout eternity. What comfort we can receive from such an amazing promise!

Look at Hebrew 9:1-28. How is Jesus better than the priesthood of Aaron and the Levites?

. . . .

Now read the conclusion of this comparison, Hebrews 10:19-25. Our hearts and our interactions with others will be changed because of our relationship with Jesus. Our prayer life can give us confidence, not only in our prayers, but in our witnessing and our service. We can know for sure our sins are forgiven, living free and living loved.

Continue memorizing *Hebrews 10:23 - "Let us hold on to the confession of our hope without wavering, for He who promised is faithful."* Write a paraphrase of the verse:

_____

_____

_____

_____

_____

❧

Oh Lord, how magnificent is your name. I give you praise and honor for your sacrifice and your eternal priesthood. You are always interceding for me. Speaking for me when I don't even have the words. Change my heart and my life to live more confidently because of this truth. Amen.

Day 5 - Conclusion

Read Hebrews 6:17-20 and Hebrews 7:1-17 and 7:1-3.

How is Jesus the best High Priest?

How is Jesus better than Melchizedek and the Old Testament High Priests?

What aspect of God's character has been revealed in the text?

How can you live as a confident Christian in your prayer life because of what you've studied this week?

How can you better live in daily *prayer* based on truths from Hebrews?

If you would like to study further, look up these verses on prayer:

Psalm 145

Romans 12:1-12

Philippians 4:4-9

Ephesians 6:10-20

I John 5:14-16

Try to write *Hebrews 10:23* from memory!

_____

_____

_____

_____

_____

Write your prayer to God, thanking Him for giving us Jesus as High Priest.

_____

_____

_____

_____

_____

Chapter 6

Throw Your Stick in the Fire

All to Jesus, I surrender;
All to Him I freely give;
I will ever love and trust Him,
In His presence daily live.
– Judson W. Van DeVenter

When I was eight years old, I surrendered my life to God, and I asked Jesus to be my Savior. I was baptized later that summer. When I was thirteen, there was this ritual at a Bible camp I attended. At the end of the week, we would all commit our lives to God and to show our commitment, we would throw a stick in the fire. So I did. As a sixteen-year-old girl, I dreamed about the mission field. So that summer, I was on the edge of a river in the jungles of Peru, on a short-term mission's trip, and I made the emotional decision to give up my dreams for God's—even if it meant *not* going on the mission field.

Fast forward fifteen years later, and I'm in the middle of motherhood with four small children. Back when I was sixteen, my dreams of surrendering to God didn't include dirty diapers, loneliness, and postpartum depression. My dreams had been steeped in adventure. God is teaching me the path of surrender doesn't always lead to the desert or jungles. Surrender is about simply coming to Jesus.

"Come to me, all who labor and are heavy laden,
and I will give you rest."
– Matthew 11:28

Coming to Jesus has everything with surrender. A surrender of our will. Our desires. Our strength. We empty ourselves. We recognize and come to Jesus with open hands. We pour out the little we have so we may fill ourselves with all that He is.

What does daily surrender look like? It means I wake up each morning and say, "I'm okay with interruptions." I'm a planner-loving control freak of a girl. I love to have my lists and detailed plans for the day. But life doesn't work that way. Whether you have children or not, we all face interruptions. The only thing I can count on every day is that things won't go the way I planned. Surrendering to the reality of life is the first step to a life of daily living.

Daily surrender means I lay the burdens of yesterday at the foot of the cross. Those moments you want to take back—leave them at the feet of Jesus' forgiveness. Christ died for my shame and it will not benefit me to pick it up and carry it around.

Everyday surrender means changing. No one likes to change—especially someone like me! If I am to surrender, I must let go of how I used to do things. I must forget the old ways and invite Jesus in to teach me a new way. If I believe my God is sovereign and in control of my life, then I can be okay with surrendering my plans to Him. God is not just in control of my destiny but also my ordinary day.

It is easy to surrender to God during an emotional church service or at the beginning of something hard. The surrender during the "mountaintop moments" of life is not the type of surrender God is asking of us. Surrendering to God on an everyday basis is the request. It requires mental activity. It requires trust.

The beauty of surrender is what we gain when we surrender. So many people dwell on what they *lose* when they surrender to Christ. We gain so much more when we give our lives to Him! This week we will focus on Romans 12 to discover what we gain when we daily surrender. Surrender is meant for the daily—sometimes the hourly. Sometimes we submit our plans to God in the beautiful hours of morning, but by late afternoon our resolve is weakened and we are snappy and irritable. May we remember the surrender is never complete.

Growing up, I went to this amazing camp for a week in the summer. One of my last years attending, they began a ritual for the older campers. We would have a bonfire at the end of the week, which had been full of laughter and fun and full of Bible teaching and instruction. Full of practical lessons and challenges. Full of camp food and living in a cabin. We were unplugged and undistracted. A challenge to follow God was issued on the last night. We sang the songs of conviction and heard the words of life. Our emotions were at an all-time high. I found it easy to surrender to God's path for my life. Nothing is wrong with making an emotional decision to follow Christ. Nothing is wrong with looking back on a big night like that and saying, "Yes, I've surrendered to whatever God has planned for me."

It is quite a different thing to wake up on a Tuesday morning at the age of thirty-three and look in the mirror and say, "I surrender all to Christ." We can have the mountaintop moments, but true surrender is getting up every day and saying, I *surrender this day to Christ. I lay down my expectations. I accept the interruptions. I plan for things not to go as planned."* When I lay down my own desires, I can let God guide me. I can serve others freely. My life can reflect the peace God promises!

O God, I surrender my day to you. Not my tomorrows but today. I give you these few hours to interrupt my life for the service of others. May I find peace and joy today in surrendering to you. Amen.

Day 1 – Prepare

Read Romans 1:1. Who wrote the book of Romans? What style was it written? To whom was it written?

Paul's letter to the Romans is full of doctrine. From the origin of sin, to Christ's atonement, to our interactions with others, this book covers all of the topics a Christian might face, even in today's world. Read Romans 1:16 for Paul's declaration at the beginning of the letter. Write it here:

_____

_____

_____

_____

_____

_____

_____

_____

The first eleven chapters of Romans deals primarily with salvation and faith. Paul describes in details the inner workings of faith and our salvation. Romans 12 is the beginning of his practical advice to the Christians in Rome. In my translation, Romans 12:1 begins with, "Therefore, brothers, by the mercies of God…." The word "therefore" means: because of everything I've said in the previous chapters, this is what you should do.

Because of our faith and salvation, what are we to do with our lives, according to Romans 12:1-2?

Based on just what you've read today, what do you think the author's purpose for writing Romans 12 might have been?

Start memorizing *Romans 12:1 - "I appeal to you therefore, brothers, by the mercies of God, to present your bodies as a living sacrifice, holy and acceptable to God, which is your spiritual worship."* Let's write it out today!

_____

_____

_____

_____

_____

Write out a prayer asking God to help you surrender your life to Him, even just for today.

_____

_____

_____

_____

Day 2 – Read

Read Romans 12 again. What did Paul encourage the believers to do?

What did he say ***not*** to do? In other words, how are believers different from non-believers, or "the world"?

In Romans 12:9-21, Paul encourages the believers to act in certain ways. He gives a list of actions and attitudes for Christians to have. Today, read through these verses and write down all of the action-words you can find.

These phrases remind me of Proverbs. The book of Proverbs is written in short, action-packed verses. We are going to do a little studying later in the week to compare Proverbs 3 with Romans 12:9-12. For now, just read Proverbs 3. What is the chapter mostly about?

Continue memorizing *Romans 12:1 - "I appeal to you therefore, brothers, by the mercies of God, to present your bodies as a living sacrifice, holy and acceptable to God, which is your spiritual worship."* Write it on a card to hang somewhere in your house.

Write out a prayer asking God to help you develop a spirit of humility.

Day 3 – A Little Deeper

In this section of Romans, the author lists some ways surrender might look in our everyday life. What can you discover from Romans 12:3-8 about surrender? What should the heart attitude be, behind our life of sacrifice?

Paul lists some spiritual gifts. What are they?

With each spiritual gift Paul lists, he always lists a way to live out the gift. With prophecy, it must align with scripture. With leading, it must be done in diligence, and when showing mercy, one must do it with a cheerful heart. Paul emphasizes the fact of surrender and service is a heart issue just as much as an outward action. Humility seems to be theme of everything Paul lists here. Humility is the key to surrender. Read Romans 12:3. How should a Christian think of himself/herself?

Read through the list of actions Paul lists in Romans 12:9-21 again. You wrote down yesterday a list of these actions. What theme or heart attitude do you see here? Remember, repeated readings benefit your study so much! Today you might see something you didn't see yesterday.

Continue memorizing *Romans 12:1 - "Appeal to you therefore, brothers, by the mercies of God, to present your bodies as alining sacrifice, holy and acceptable to God, which is your spiritual worship."* Say the verse aloud three times.

Oh Lord God, your idea of surrender and my idea of surrender might be two separate things. I pray you will help my heart be characterized by humility. Amen.

Day 4 – Your Turn

Today I want you to compare Proverbs 3 and Romans 12. Read Proverbs 1:1-7. Why is Proverbs called the "wisdom book"?

Let's look at how Proverbs describes our acts of surrender compared to Paul's list. Record how Proverbs words the same commands from Romans 12.

Reference	Romans	Proverbs
Romans 12:9	*Let love be genuine.*	Proverbs 3:3
	Hold fast to what is good	Proverbs 3:18
Romans 12:10	*Love one another*	Proverbs 10:12
Romans 12:12	*Rejoice in hope*	Proverbs 10:28
Romans 12:13	*Contribute to the needs of other Christians*	Proverbs 31:9
	Seek to show hospitality	Proverbs 3:27
Romans 12:16	*Live in harmony (peace) with others*	Proverbs 12:20
	Do not be haughty (proud)	Proverbs 29:23
	Associate with the lowly	Proverbs 3:28
	Never be wise in your own sight	Proverbs 29:11
Romans 12:19	*Never avenge yourself*	Proverbs 20:22

Work on memorizing *Romans 12:1* - *"I appeal to you therefore, brothers, by the mercies of God, to present your bodies as a living sacrifice, holy and acceptable to God, which is your spiritual worship."* Write a paraphrase of the verse:

_____

_____

_____

_____

_____

⸙

Oh Lord I pray you will do a work in my heart as I live in wisdom and in line with your Word. I pray you will guide me into daily surrender.

Day 5 – Conclusion

Surrender looks different for different people. Our spiritual gifts will look different for different people. We cannot compare the way we surrender to the way the girl on the other side of social media surrenders. Something common for both of us is our heart attitude. It should be one of humility.

What aspect of God's character has been revealed in the text?

How should the truths from Romans 12 play out in my daily life?

How can I better live in daily *surrender* based on truths from Romans 12?

Some truths I wish to leave you with...

1. I'm not better because of the way I surrender. As we have seen this week, surrender can take on a lot of different forms. The one common factor is humility. If my heart is humble and willing to be laid out as a living sacrifice, I can rest assured I am striving to surrender.

2. Surrendering sometimes means I have to admit I don't do everything. Just looking at the lists of spiritual gifts is overwhelming. The beautiful thing is, I don't have to do it all. And I don't have to do it all in my own strength. According to Romans 12:6 it is through grace I even have the ability to serve. Humility is again the key.

3. Using my gifts is the key to sacrifice. I will tell you, moving to an African country and living in a mud hut with a dirt floor is probably not my gift. My surrender looks different, and that's ok. I can rest in the way I surrender, even if it is different.

Try to write *Romans 12:1* from memory!

_____

_____

_____

_____

Write your prayer to God, surrendering your life to Him....

_____

_____

_____

_____

_____

Chapter 7

Pushed Into the Deep End

Appalachian summers are filled with heat and humidity. Seventy degrees feels like 90. On the really hot days, when I was a child, my mom and siblings and I would pile into the minivan and drive three minutes up the hill behind our house. Mom would park at the bottom of the hill, and my brother, sisters, and I would pack-mule it up the concrete path from the parking lot to the entrance to the city pool. Chlorine and '90s music greeted us as we walked in. The teenager behind the counter would smile and pull out our family's membership card. We dumped our snacks, towels, and blow-up rings in our usual spot: next to the baby pool but within view of the deep end.

The water, cool and blue, beckoned us to jump. My ten-year-old brother would run to the deep end and climb the high ladder to dive into the 12-foot section. I was content swimming in the shallows. Even though I was a good swimmer, the dark blue water frightened me. I didn't like to swim where I couldn't see the bottom.

Sometimes my brother and his friends would sneak up behind me and push me into the deep end. I never found it humorous. I was always mad about it. I didn't like the feeling of not touching, and panic creeped into my heart as the water lapped beside my neck, seeping into my mouth. I struggled to breathe, and even though the wall was close by, I hated the feeling of not being in control.

I wanted to know what I was jumping into. I'm a planner. During our adoption, I had a plan. I was pretty sure I was prepared for the unknown and had even planned for it. I thought I was ready for whatever God's plan was for our family. But I wasn't. I remember the feelings of drowning. The rushing water of uncertainty creeping up and over into my comfortable life. When our daughter's special need was more significant than we had planned for, it was like jumping into the deep end all over again. It wrecked all of my hard work and destroyed my plans.

In the middle of my ocean of fear, I couldn't see Him. I couldn't see a reason to hope. *One day I might see you in this but not today*, I thought. I held out my hands, empty of hope, and found a friend's hand. Community surrounded our family. We knew the waters were deep, but God had not abandoned us. Until we could touch bottom, they jumped into the water and held us up. As I walked hand in hand with my husband, friends, and family, I stopped thinking about the future.

It's funny because hope seems tied to the future. Hope was something I thought maybe you just had. As I began to search Scripture, I realized hope was something that grew. It was something that could get bigger and bigger. And it wasn't like I would suddenly have hope. The in-between seasons are sometimes a time of despair. For me, sadness led to depression. Suddenly, I lost sight of the Son. I became clouded with uncertainty, and fears began to take root in my heart, pushing out the hope. I was so focused on the unknown future that I couldn't see the daily hope.

I found myself reading Scripture, praying, and going to church, but without hope, my religion was useless. I was doing all the right things, but hope didn't show up. What if we read all of the verses? What if hope still doesn't shine through the darkness? Surely something is wrong with me. Surely I am the problem.

Hope is found in one place: God's presence. While our family was struggling to breathe again after China, we held close to the presence of God. The God we knew was still working good. The God we knew would walk through these uncertain waters with us.

How do we let in the light of hope when our world is full of silence and darkness? Stay close to Jehovah. Stay close to what we know. Stay close to truth. Light will follow. One day I was in our church's nursery. I glanced over at a little girl who was about seven months old, the same amount of time our daughter had been home. I noticed her head and back were straight. She sat up and made gurgling sounds. Her eyes made perfect eye contact. I looked away, embarrassed and sad. My two-and-a-half-year-old daughter could do none of those. It hurt. I almost cried. It was hard to see other children make progress more quickly while mine seemed "stuck."

When parenting a child with so many unknowns, who is behind physically, mentally, verbally, and developmentally, it can be overwhelming. You wake up each morning to routines and coping mechanisms. Survival becomes the norm. You live from one meltdown to the next. Sometimes your own tears mix with theirs.

So I began having hope in just today. I started enjoying all of the things she could do right then. Loving the things she loved. Giving her extra time during the day to just cuddle. Or extra kisses and hugs. There had been months of loneliness for my sweet girl, so I began to dwell on the present. The future was (still is) so unknown. The past was unknown. But it became okay once I began to have hope in the present. Hope not in the future or in the past but in right now.

Daily hope isn't about feeling a certain way all of the time. It's okay to have hope one minute and find the tears falling into your coffee later. Hope is about staying close to God, letting in the light, and choosing to trust. What we believe about God's Word is directly related to our hope!

And having hope is a beautiful thing. Not because all of the pieces fit together. No, the pieces of my heart are still very much broken. They are scattered all over the floor, and I can't make sense of my story sometimes. But God is making it beautiful...because I am looking up. My daughter's story will be just as beautiful because I know my God.

When you can't hear a thing
There are no words to sing
You keep your heart where it's safe
But the world is a silent place

Stay with me
You'll be surprised
There's a world of color
Beyond black and white
Open your eyes
Let in the light
You'll see when you stay with me
– JJ Heller, "Stay"

You will be surprised when you find the light. Trust in what you know. Actively believe in the truth from God's Word to live a life of daily hope. One of the best books of the Bible in which to find hope is Psalms. I challenge you to read through the entire book. Take one chapter a day, and with 150 chapters, you can do it in less than a year, even if you don't do it every day. It will take less than five minutes to read most of the chapters. We will spend the next six days looking at hope through the lens of Psalm 119, and how God's Word is just enough hope for today.

Oh Lord of our HOPE, give me hope today. Just for today I need to see a little light. I need to see your hand, even if today is clouded with darkness and rain. Let me see YOU. Amen

---

Day 1 – Prepare

I am so excited to start this week with you. Hope is something we all long for but seldom find. I've lived a year in the deep end of the pool, learning to swim in the murky waters. Many days I would wake up, feeling despair and discouraged. I looked to the only place I could, God's Word. As we study daily hope, I want to take you to Psalm 119. Don't be alarmed, we won't be studying the entire chapter (all 150 verses!) I've picked a few sections for us to focus on, which speak specifically to having hope. Today we will look at an overview of Psalm 119.

> I want you to do some research. You can look online, in commentaries, or your study Bible. Answer the following questions:

First, find out who all is mentioned as the possible author of Psalm 119. I'll give you a hint: we can't know for sure. Just find out what you can about the author and his possible audience.

How is the psalm arranged? What can you discover conferring the layout and pattern of Psalm 119?

Briefly read through Psalm 119:1-1-8. What are the various words used for the Bible, God's Word?

What is the obvious subject of Psalm 119? Describe how the author feels about this subject.

Start memorizing *Psalm 119:114 - "You are my hiding place and my shield; I hope in your word." Write it out here.

_____

_____

_____

_____

_____

Oh Lord, I give you praise for your excellent words. May they seep into my heart this week as I study. Renew in me a spirit of hope. Amen.

Day 2 – Read

Today we will read the various sections of Psalm 119 dealing with God's Word and hope. For each section write any "action" words you see in this section (incline, long for, comfort, kept, sought, etc.). What is the psalmist doing with God's Word? How does he respond and interact with God's Word?

Psalm 119:33-48

Psalm 119:114-120

Psalm 119:145-152

Look up any words you do not understand. Look up words that are repeated. Make notes of what you find in both a dictionary *and* a thesaurus.

Continue memorizing *Psalm 119:114 - "You are my hiding place and my shield; I hope in your word."* Write it on a card to hang somewhere in your house.

Write out a prayer asking God to help you develop a deep love for His Word.

_____

_____

_____

_____

_____

_____

_____

Day 3 – A Little Deeper

Now look at each section again in Psalm 119. What happens when the psalmist (and we) do these things from the previous question? What will we have if we incline, long for, and trust God's Word? Hope is one answer, but will we gain anything else from reading, learning, and trusting in God's Word?

Psalm 119:33-48

Psalm 119:114-120

Psalm 119:145-152

What do these other verses say about God's Word?

Isaiah 40:8

Matthew 7:24

Hebrews 4:12

2 Timothy 3:16-17

Continue memorizing *Psalm 119:114 - "You are my hiding place and my shield; I hope in your word."* Say the verse aloud three times.

Oh God of the True Word, I pray you will help me to trust your Word more. I know it is the hope I need, no matter what today brings. Lead me in daily hope as I cling to your promises. Amen.

Day 4 – Your Turn

God's Word is the perfect source of hope for our lives. Practically speaking, how do we find hope, especially in difficult times? What does Psalm 119:15-16 say? Write it here:

What does the word "mediate" mean? Look it up and make notes of what you find in both a dictionary *and* a thesaurus.

Read Psalm119:11 and Psalm 119:97-105. What does the author do with God's Word?

It is vital we start to memorize and meditate on God's Word. We can believe God's Word, but if we truly trust the promises, we have to know what they are in times of trouble! Today, I want you to pick one passage from the list below to begin to commit to memory after this study is over. Write it on a piece of paper, notecard, or your journal. You can write it on the back pages of this study if you want. Begin right away, after you have finished, to memorize the passage.

Psalm 3

Psalm 46

Psalm 147

Romans 5:1-5

James 1:1-5

I Peter 1:3-6

Work on memorizing *Psalm 119:114 - "You are my hiding place and my shield; I hope in your word"* Write a paraphrase of the verse:

_____

_____

_____

_____

_____

Oh Lord, I pray you will help me be diligent in memorizing and meditating on your word. In your promises do I find hope for the future. Amen.

Day 5 – Conclusion

Let's review. What is the theme of Psalm 119?

What aspect of God's character has been revealed in the text?

How does understanding that characteristic of God change the way you should think and act?

How can I better live in daily *hope* based on truths from Psalm 119?

What passage did you choose yesterday? Write the first verse here:

_____

_____

_____

_____

_____

_____

_____

Try to write *Psalm 119:114* from memory!

_____

_____

_____

_____

Write your prayer to God, thanking Him for the hope in His Word.

_____

_____

_____

_____

Chapter 8
The Burden of Praise

The day God began teaching me about living daily was the day I discovered a deep fear. I was sitting on a hot bus and traveling at a snail's pace in the heart of Guangzhou, China. I sat beside the window looking at the people below on the streets. They were cooking in the open air, standing in doorways of shops, and walking along the sidewalks. Children were bundled in three layers, even in 80-degree weather. I glanced at my husband next to me holding our daughter. She was still withdrawing, still grieving. Fear began to creep over me, making it hard to breathe. What would her future be? What would my future be? Would the future be predictable at all anymore?

So many unanswered questions, some still unanswered a year and a half later, but I remember the ride and the tears underneath the surface. Tears from exhaustion. Tears from physically missing my other little ones. Mostly I had tears from fear—a fear of the future. Fear threatened to ruin the day of shopping and fun planned for us. I decided to shove down the fear, swallow my tears, and walk through the oasis of Shamain Island—the Spanish moss and the architecture that resembled what I pictured Savannah, Georgia to be like. We moved in and out of the streets. I decided to soak in that day, ignoring the fear and continuing to move forward—even if it was just for that one day.

After coming home from China, we suffered through the fog of jet lag and began putting our family together again piece by piece. It wasn't the same as before, and the fear returned. I pushed it down again and again until the fear of the future overwhelmed me like a flood. Suddenly, I was in the middle of an ocean of adoption blues and desperate for relief.

In the middle of my ocean of fear, I couldn't praise Him. *One day I might praise you, God, but not today,* I prayed. I held out my hands, empty of praise, and found Him. Ready to reach for me. Ready to wait for me. Ready to change my heart when I wasn't even seeking the growth—I wanted to just survive.

I'm still learning this messy thing of daily praise. I write to you from a place of broken praise. I see now I never had it together. I see now I never was just a "good girl" needing a little grace. The Lord revealed the depths of my sin. My God has allowed the darkness to seep in to reveal how brilliantly His light shines—and that praise doesn't have to wait.

One day at a time, I'm learning to praise Him. Praise Him when my heart just isn't feeling it. Praise Him when my life feels so out of control. Praise Him for the good. Praise Him for the hard. Praise Him for who He is. As my eyes turn away from my own desperation, I see the fullness of Christ and the steadfast love and daily mercy available to me. The more I praise Him, the more I see Him.

"Take my yoke upon you, and learn of me."
– Matthew 11:29

"The fact that the peace and the light and the joy of God are there {in a Christian's life} is proof that the burden is there too… The only way to know the strength of God is to take the yoke of Jesus upon us and learn of Him."
– Oswald Chambers [13]

The burden of praise is when we lay our own heartaches down at the foot of the cross and we pick up the yoke of Christ. We choose to live in the daily. To walk in the ordinary. To see Him in the everyday moments. Praise is about looking up. And when we look up, no matter the season, we find Jesus there, holding us all along. The broken road to praise doesn't have to be fixed first. We can walk along the pieces, picking our way through the rubble. Making mistakes. Choosing praise.

The daily turning of my eyes to Jesus means seeking Him in His Word. I may not be able to utter the words, but my heart can choose. My mind can make the choice to praise Jesus. The goodness and light of His promises are worthy of praise, no matter how my heart feels.

As we study praise, may we realize praise doesn't have to wait. It can start today. I'm still learning creative ways to keep praise first in my mind, especially when my heart is heavy with the guilt of the past and the fear of the future. Instead of waiting to praise God, thinking, "One day I will praise you," I'm thinking, "No matter the sorrow of yesterday and the fear of tomorrow—I will praise You."

Nothing says Pentecostal to this Baptist girl more than praise hands. Only at concerts or at friends' churches did I get to experience the praise hands while growing up. When I say "experience," I mean watching. My hands just didn't naturally lift high in worship. Praise hands are amazing. It is such a beautiful picture of a heart posture. But I don't need praise hands to praise God.

Many times, standing during Sunday morning worship, my heart will swell with thanksgiving and awe at the love and grace of my Father. In those moments, my heart lifts up its own invisible hands to the Father. It is a soul praise. A praise to God with no words or outward posture. I listen to the words of a song or the beautiful music, letting the goodness of God soak my very being, and my heart rejoices with the glory of God.

I've also stood up singing on a Sunday morning weighed down with heartache and grief, unable to utter a single word or even read the words on the screen. During the time of praise, my heart is bent low in deep sorrow, not even able to see the goodness of Him. In those moments, the Holy Spirit slides into the seat next to me and lets me praise God with unspoken words. The Spirit speaks for me, interceding before the Father, voicing the needs I cannot.

Praise isn't about joy. Praise isn't an emotion or something we have but something we do. Praise isn't about singing the songs on Sunday morning. Praise is what we lift to the Father, no matter the outward position. It is an act of the will. It is the response of the heart. It is both together. Praise is something God has called us to do during our season of growth. Praise is the first step we can take toward growth. Look up.

O Heavenly King, may I lift my eyes to praise you. No matter how I am feeling, may I lean into your faithfulness and always find a reason to praise you. Amen.

Day 1 – Prepare

Read the beginning (before verse one) in Psalm 90. What does it say? Write it here:

Who wrote Psalm 90? Write down everything you know about the author.

Is there a heading at the beginning of Psalm 91? Do you think it is possible for the author of Psalm 91 to be the same author of Psalm 90? Why?

What word do you see in Psalm 90:1 AND in Psalm 91:1? Look especially in the English Standard Version of the Bible.

Write down the definition of "dwell" here:

Moses is thought to be the author of Psalm 90, 91, and even 92. We will focus primarily on Psalm 91 and Psalm 92 this week. Moses led the people out of slavery from Egypt, set up the laws, and recorded the Ten Commandments. He was called a "friend of God" and was regarded as one of Israel's greatest leaders. He is believed to be the author of Genesis, Exodus, Leviticus, and Deuteronomy. At the beginning of Deuteronomy, Moses begins to speak to the people of Israel after a great battle. In this battle, God fought for them and they defeated nations much more powerful then themselves. The Israelites were about to enter into the promised land. What does Moses say to the people in Deuteronomy 6:1-9? Summarize Moses' words and paraphrase them.

Keep this in mind, the theme of Moses' charge to the people of Israel, as we study these psalms of praise this week. Start memorizing Psalm 92:1 - *"It is good to give thanks to the LORD, to sing praises to your name, O Most High."* Write it out here.

_____

_____

_____

_____

Oh Lord, I give you praise for your excellent words. May they seep into my heart this week as I study. Begin a work of daily praise in my heart today. Amen.

Day 2 – Read

Read Psalm 91 again. Look up the following passages. How do
they relate to Psalm 91?

Psalm 59:16-17

Psalm 71:1-4

Psalm 144:1-4

What will happen if someone makes God his "dwelling place"?

What synonyms can you find for "dwell" and "abide"?

In Psalm 92:14-16, God begins to speak to the author. Write God's words here:

_____

_____

_____

_____

_____

_____

_____

_____

_____

Read Psalm 91:1-2 and Psalm 91:9-10. What does it mean to "abide" and "dwell" in God's presence? How do we do that?

Continue memorizing Psalm 92:1 - *"It is good to give thanks to the LORD, to sing praises to your name, O Most High."* Write it on a card to hang somewhere in your house.

Write out a prayer asking God to help you abide more fully in His presence.

_____

_____

_____

_____

Day 3 – A Little Deeper

Read the account of the defeat of two powerful kings by Moses in Joshua 12:1-6. Although it is recorded in Joshua, these events happened in Numbers 21:33-35. Now read Psalm 91:7-8. What even more significance can you find in these verses penned by Moses?

In Psalm 90-91 we see a description of God. Summarize these two chapters in just a few sentences.

In Psalm 92 we find the response to God's character. What does the heading (before verse one) say in Psalm 92?

The Sabbath was a day to rest and a day to celebrate God's provision and protection by reflecting on His Word. When does Psalm 92:1-2 say we should praise God?

How should we praise God according to Psalm 92:3-4?

And why should we praise God in Psalm 92:5-11?

What is the picture the author uses to describe the person who lives in daily praise?

Do a little research. What can you discover in a study Bible or online about the Biblical city of Lebanon? Read here: http://www.biblestudytools.com/

dictionary/lebanon/. An interesting fact about Lebanon is it was the place where the King Solomon found the lumber to build the temple. Read more here: http://www.bibleplaces.com/cedar-of-lebanon/. What significance is there in Moses saying we will grow like trees from Lebanon?

Continue memorizing Psalm 92:1 - *"It is good to give thanks to the LORD, to sing praises to your name, O Most High."* Say the verse aloud three times.

O God, let me sing to you today a song of praise. You make me dwell in safety. Even when circumstances are swirling around me, there is peace in your presence. I give you thanks for your wonderful works! Amen.

Day 4 – Your Turn

What does it mean "it is good to give thanks" in this section? How many times does the author give praise or thanks to God in this passage?

The name "LORD" appears several times in this section. Look up that word in a study Bible. What is the Hebrew translation of this name for God? What does it mean, historically?

LORD is God's name He uses to describe a personal relationship. How do we live better in daily praise when we know God as a personal God?

Write a paraphrase of both Psalm 91 & Psalm 92.

Read Psalm 92:1 again. Does life always "feel" good? How is it **good** to praise God, even when we are hurting, lonely, or afraid?

Work on memorizing *Psalm 92:1 - "It is good to give thanks to the LORD, to sing praises to your name, O Most High."* Write a paraphrase of the verse:

_____

_____

_____

_____

O Lord, how I long to know you more. The more I know about you the more I can praise you daily. Amen.

Day 5 – Conclusion

What two characteristics of God are found in Psalm 92:2-3? What about Psalm 91? What character trait of God is evident in this psalm?

How does understanding that characteristic of God change the way you should think and act?

How can I better live in daily *praise* based on truths from Psalm 91 &92?

How can you begin each morning praising God? One suggestion would be to begin a praise journal. Each day, spend a few minutes writing down a few things to give God thanks or praise for. Another idea would be to sing praise songs on your way to work or as you cook breakfast. If you play an instrument, set aside some time each week to just play and sing praise to God.

How can you end each night praising God? Suggestions include writing in your praise journal before bed, reading a Psalm before you go to sleep, or just simply singing a short praise song in your heart while you brush your teeth. Be creative and be practical.

Today I am going to live in daily praise by...

Try to write *Psalm 92:1* from memory!

_____

_____

_____

_____

Write your prayer to God, giving Him praise for who He is and what He has done!

_____

_____

_____

_____

_____

_____

Chapter 9

Too Much, Never Enough

When the Lord says He will equip those He calls, He might not mean He is equipping me for something big or something grand and glorious. Maybe what He is equipping me for is something ordinary. Small. Invisible. I will have mountaintop moments. I will feel grand and maybe even get to do one grand thing in my lifetime. I will not be remembered in the hearts of those I love for my one big thing. I will be remembered, when I am gone, for the little things. I will be missed for my hugs. I will be missed for my smile and laughter. I will be missed for the *everyday* me, not the grand me.

So today I live knowing the glorious work of love is not invisible. It may not be noticed or appreciated, but the glorious work is seen by a glorious God. When I do all of the laundry in one day and stand back, no one applauds with loud cheering. When my floors are freshly mopped, the thanks I usually get is ketchup spilled on them.

Not only does God see my work in the ordinary and daily, but He sees <u>me</u>. He placed me here—not on the mountaintop of achievement, success, or fame, but in the present. He placed me here because He is here.

A present living means to be healed from our past. Daily forgiveness is ours for the taking. We trust God and have hope He is working towards a good future. A present living means we surrender, love, and rest in knowing our God is enough. We can live in truth, grace, and prayer because our God is a God of the here and now.

God is our refuge and strength, a very present help in trouble.
Psalm 46:1

Never mind the waves of uncertainty. Never mind the fears of the future or the guilt of the past—our God is bigger. When the psalmist speaks about the LORD of hosts, picture a God in charge of angel armies. The word "host" literally means hundreds and hundreds of angels. Our God is so powerful that He commands legions of angels. What does this powerful God do? He is with us. Close. Beside us. Like a friend who sits on the couch and holds our hand while we weep together. A companion so close we cannot help but know. A powerful God is personal.

Forget the mountains crumbling. The God of Jacob is near. Who was Jacob? Oh, you know, the man who used his mother to lie to his father so he could steal from his brother. The man who fought God's will in his life—until God won. The God of Jacob is a personal God. And what does this personal God do? He is our refuge. A tower. Not just to hide us away but to protect us. A refuge. A place of safety. Seems like we would need a pretty powerful God to rescue us and provide refuge. It would seem contradictory to think a personal God could be so powerful.

Yet here we have it, the key to living in the present: **Our powerful God is personal, and our personal God is powerful.** We need to know He is big enough to handle all of the waves and winds of life. We also need to know we aren't alone on the seas. He is right beside us in the boat… holding us close…letting us rest in His hope and grace. God's presence is the place to start when we begin to live in the daily.

Our daughter taught me to live in the daily. When we stepped off the airplane on March 19, 2015, I wrapped my arms around my other little ones and stepped into a new life. I stepped into daily living. I began to hang on to truth, just enough for today. I believed what I knew, not what I felt. I started to let God's promises be my anchor. Many days were spent weeping. Sometimes wishing for the past. Sometimes fearing the future. So many questions, and I thought the unknowns would be behind us once we brought our daughter home.

As I began to search Scripture for who I knew God to be and what He promised, I began to sense His presence. Not overnight. Many months later, I am still living in the daily. I am still seeking satisfaction. When I find my satisfaction in the Rock, there is indeed honey enough for today.

O the river it rushes to madness
And the water it spreads like sadness
And there's no high ground
And there's no high ground
Closer to the danger and the rolling deep
Closer to the run and the losing streak
And what brings us to our knees
– Sara Groves, "Floodplain" [15]

O God of my presence, come near and be a God who is big enough to cover me in these hard seasons. May I find you a refuge when the waters spread into sadness. Bring me to you, here on my knees. Help me to live in today. Amen.

Day 1 – Prepare

Read Psalm 46, before verse one. Who wrote this passage? We will study the author a little more in detail on day three. For today, let's focus on just reading through the psalm to get the bigger picture.

How does the Psalmist describe God in this passage?

What does God do?

Who is God, according to just this section?

What phrase do you see repeated?

The word "selah" means rest or pause. Look at Psalm 46:3 and 7. What is the significance of pausing after this phrase?

What do you think the author's purpose for writing might have been? Be brief. You will answer this question again at the end of the week.

Write a paraphrase (in your own words) of the passage.

Start memorizing Psalm 46:1 - *"God is our refuge and strength, a very present help in trouble."*

Write it out here.

_____

_____

_____

_____

_____

_____

❧

Oh Lord, I give you praise for your excellent words. May they seep into my heart this week as I study. Begin a work of daily praise in my heart today. Amen.

Day 2 – Read

Read Psalm 46 again and write out the entire psalm today.

What verses stand out?

_____

_____

What words stand out to you?

_____

_____

How is God described?

_____

_____

How is life described?

_____

_____

What is the response to God's presence in Psalm 46:10?

_____

_____

Continue memorizing Psalm 46:1 - *"God is our refuge and strength, a very present help in trouble."* Write it on a card to hang somewhere in your house.

Write out a prayer asking God to help you trust Him as your refuge.

_____

_____

_____

_____

_____

Day 3 – A Little Deeper

Let's do a little research on the author of Psalm 46. Read I Chronicles 6:31-38. We have a list of the "sons of Korah" here in Chronicles. Whose name is mentioned as the "son of" in verse 34 who is also found in I Samuel 1:1?

Some believe this is the same man. Who was this man and who was his son, according to I Samuel 1:20?

What did some of these men do during David's reign as king (1 Chronicles 6:31-32)?

Some believe these men were also the authors of other psalms. Aseph was also thought to be one of the sons of Korah. See 1 Chronicles 25:1-2. Read Psalm 73:23-28. How does it relate to Psalm 46?

Look up the Psalm 73:1, 23-28. Who wrote this psalm? How does it relate to Psalm 46?

How do these verses echo the thoughts of Psalm 46?

Psalm 59:16-17

Jeremiah 16:19-21

Make a list of all of the things God DOES (look for action words like "help" or "makes").

Make a list of all of the things God IS (look for the word "is").

Continue memorizing Psalm 46:1 - *"God is our refuge and strength, a very present help in trouble."* Say the verse aloud three times.

―――――――――❧❦――――――――――

O God, I give you praise for the wonderful things you do and the things you are. May my heart be at peace and find joy in knowing you are truly enough. Amen.

―――――――――❧❦――――――――――

Day 4 – Your Turn

Psalm 46:1 says in the ESV version: *"God is our refuge and strength, a very present help in trouble."* What do think the word "present" means? What does it mean God is our "very present help"?

What do you think Psalm 46 means. Write a paraphrase.

The Psalms use pictures to help convey literary images. If you were to draw, color, or paint a picture of Psalm 46, what would it look like? Use either art or words to convey the meaning behind Psalm 46.

What does "be still" mean in Psalm 46:10? The Hebrew word, וּפְרַ ה, means to relax. To keep calm, stop striving. How do we rest, according to the rest of Psalm 46:10?

When we know God is God, our hearts find the ability to relax. I am learning our daughter's diagnosis wasn't what we would have said "yes" to when we started this journey. If we had heard the term for what she has, we would have said no. God is still good. God is still God. Knowing more of who He is gives my heart a way to work through the idea that our family will now look different than I had pictured. He wanted her in our family, so I believe He hid the true diagnosis until I could fall in love with her, no matter what. What an amazingly good God!? I need only be still and trust.

What circumstances are happening in your life right now in which you need to trust God and be still?

Work on memorizing *Psalm 46:1 - "God is our refuge and strength, a very present help in trouble."*

Write a paraphrase of the verse:

_____

_____

_____

_____

O Lord, how I long to know you more. The more I know about you the more I can rest in who you are. Amen.

Day 5 – Conclusion

What are the names of God used in Psalm 46?

Based on His names, what He does, and who He is, how would you describe God?

What is the response to God's character in this section?

How can I better live in daily *presence* based on truths from Psalm 46?

What do these verses reveal about God's presence?

Psalm 16:11

Psalm 95:2

Isaiah 63:9

How should we respond when we realize God is ever-present with us? His presence brings what to our lives?

Try to write *Psalm 46:1* from memory!

_____

_____

_____

_____

Write your prayer to God, thanking Him for His presence with you...

_____

_____

_____

_____

Conclusion

"They who wait for the LORD…shall walk and not faint."
– Isaiah 40:31

We always give the children of Israel a hard time. God had just parted the Red Sea. It was the pinnacle of their redemption. They had just witnessed a miracle. Three days later, we find them complaining. But God responds to their complaining with a promise to provide.

Exodus 16:4, 9, and 12 say, *"Then the LORD said to Moses, 'Behold, I am about to rain bread from heaven for you, and the people shall go out and gather a day's portion every day, that I may test them, whether they will walk in my law or not…Then Moses said…'Come near before the LORD, for he has heard your grumbling…and in the morning you shall be filled with bread. Then you shall know that I am the LORD your God.'"*

The "manna" was a test. God asked them to trust Him. To believe He would provide, every day. More than just providing for their hungry stomachs, God was going to provide healing for their souls. He told Moses it was a test. Manna is about living in the present. Will we trust God? Daily living means God will be enough for today, and tomorrow we will have enough too.

The manna became more than just their food. The manna was a living, daily reminder of God's provision. A miracle every day. God pays attention to the daily. God could have given them all the manna they would need for the next forty years on that first day. Instead, He allowed them to live one day at a time. They were not to rush ahead and gather for the future. Today we have God's Word. It is our manna, our portion for today. As we study the Bible, we find God provides just what we need.

God has called us to walk one day at a time. And as we walk, He provides.

We do not want to walk; we want to run. Run fast. Run ahead. We don't want to wait on paperwork. Or deadlines. Or signatures. We do not want to wait for approvals or court dates. We don't want to wait on treatments or test results. We do not wait for children to come home. We want to run ahead to the future.

Walking involves His presence. When your life is not rushed but relaxed, you can see more of God's presence in your life. You will see Him in the small things. In the details. The times He walks before you, making the path clear. The Lord is God, and He is near. We need only look for Him. As we've discovered, He is found right here, in the pages of Scripture.

Notes:

[1] Chambers, Oswald. My Utmost for His Highest: Selections for the Year. New York: Dodd, Mead, 1935. Print.

[2] Chambers

[3] Smith, Hannah Whitall. The Christian's Secret of a Happy Life. Westwood, NJ: Revell, 1952. Print.

[4] Lloyd-Jones, Sally, and Jago. The Story of God's Love for You. Grand Rapids, MI: Zondervan, 2015. Print.

[5] Chambers

[6] H., Spurgeon C. The Treasury of David. N.p.: Virginia, n.d. Print. Pg 172.

[7] Murray, Andrew. Abiding in Christ. Minneapolis, MN: Bethany House, 2003. Print.

[8] Murray

[9] Miles, Austin C. In the Garden Alone. http://www.hymnary.org/hymn/UMH/314.

[10] Lloyd.

[11] Chambers.

[12] Lemme, Helen H. Turn Your Eyes Upon Jesus. http://www.hymnary.org/text/o_soul_are_you_weary_and_troubled

[13] Chambers.

[14] Groves, Sara. Enough. http://www.songlyrics.com/sara-groves/

[15] Groves, Sara. Floodplain. http://www.songlyrics.com/sara-groves/.

FOR FURTHER BIBLE STUDY:

www.sarahefrazer.com

Sarah lives her life with an amazing husband and four little ones (one adopted from China). Her inner-planner girl would like to say she's super efficient and has the house, homeschool, and husband all neatly organized. But she doesn't. Sarah's house is run with fuel from coffee and Jesus. She is learning how to find the thrill of walking one day at a time in the messiness of mundane. She invites you to study God's Word in your ordinary days.